The Italian Army at War
Europe 1940-43

Text: Philip Jowett
Color Plates: Dmitriy Zgonnik

Copyright © 2008
by CONCORD PUBLICATIONS CO.
B1, 10/F, Kong Nam Industrial Building
603-609 Castle Peak Road
Tsuen Wan, New Territories
Hong Kong
www.concord-publications.com

We welcome authors who can help
expand our range of books. If you
would like to submit material,
please feel free to contact us.

We are always on the look-out for new,
unpublished photos for this series.
If you have photos or slides or
information you feel may be useful to
future volumes, please send them to us
for possible future publication.
Full photo credits will be given upon
publication.

ISBN 962-361-150-1
printed in Hong Kong

Introduction

When Italy declared war on France and Great Britain on 10 June 1940, the Mediterranean nation had on paper a formidable army of 73 divisions. This impressive figure concealed one of the main weaknesses of the Italian Army, however, that each division was only two infantry regiments strong instead of the standard three regiments in all other armies. Also, in each division there was only one regiment of artillery, which compared unfavorably with other armies that had at least four artillery groups per division.

Again on paper, the Italians had an impressive armored force of several thousand tanks. Unfortunately this force was overwhelmingly made up of two-man light tanks armed with twin machineguns. Most artillery pieces were old and out of date with a large number of guns being Austro-Hungarian war booty taken as reparations in 1918. The Italians also had the disadvantage of many of its soldiers having already fought in Ethiopia in 1935-36 and Spain in 1937-39. A lot of these soldiers were thus war weary. These veterans of several conflicts had received little home leave, and so were not motivated or ready for the kind of war that was to face them in 1940-43.

The Italians did have many superb units with 12 regiments of the famous Bersaglieri light infantry and ten of Alpini, "crack" mountain troops recruited from the hardy people of Italy's mountainous regions. Some infantry divisions were regarded as elite units - for instance, the *Lupi di Toscana* (Wolves of Tuscany) were a favorite of Mussolini, while the *Gratnieri di Savoia* (Grenadiers of Savoy) had a long and illustrious history. At the start of the war Italy had 39 infantry divisions, four Alpini, two motorized, three truck transportable, two armored and two Celere light divisions at home. In Albania there were three infantry, one Alpini and one armored divisions with a further infantry division in the Aegean islands. The rest of the Italian Army, along with a large number of colonial units, was stationed in North and East Africa.

Italy's first military operation in WWII involved the invasion of southeast France along the mostly mountainous Western Alps border. With the French on the verge of defeat in June 1940 and only a few days away from capitulation, Mussolini declared war on them and Great Britain on 10 June. The Italian High Command, Commando Supremo, had envisaged a defensive strategy against France before the war and all their dispositions had to be changed in a few days at Mussolini's command. His staff tried to reason quite rightly that it would take weeks to properly organize the offensive and bring up the weaponry such as heavy artillery needed to reduce the well-built French fortifications. Mussolini would have no excuses and issued orders for the offensive to begin on 17 June, the same day France asked Germany for an armistice. This order was countermanded at the last minute, and by the time the delayed offensive was launched on 20 June, 25 infantry and alpine divisions plus a small armored element had been massed on the border.

As soon as the offensive was underway, the Italians experienced difficulties. They bogged down on a narrow front with poor weather and unexpected resistance from French alpine units making progress slow and costly. The inclement weather also meant the Italian Air Force could not give support to the offensive and the poor Italian infantry had to launch costly frontal assaults against well-prepared French positions with no air and only light artillery support. The French had also prepared well, with a series of well-sited demolitions along border passes being set off on 11 June. These demolitions held up the Italians and stopped a lot of support elements from getting to the front before the end of the fighting. However, the Italians did manage to occupy the villages of Lanslebourg and Termignon in the Arc Valley before the French surrender on 24 June.

The campaign in the Alps could hardly be described as a great success even though small gains were trumpeted by the Fascist propaganda machine. At the same time, the divisions fighting along the Cote d'Azur, the southern French coast, also made little progress in their quest to take the city of Nice before the French surrender. Only about two thirds of the town of Menton, just 8km over the border, had been captured before the armistice. Attempts to take the well-defended city of Nice with its 472 field guns (including many heavy types) came to nothing with three Italian divisions stopped by the city's defenses despite their bravery. Italian losses in the four-day campaign were relatively heavy with more than 600 killed and 2361 wounded, as well as 600 missing.

In many instances the Italians had tried their best in difficult circumstances to carry out Mussolini's orders, but French defenses proved too strong and only a long campaign of attrition would have reduced them. The severe weather during the campaign also badly affected the Italians, this being graphically illustrated by the 2151 cases of frostbite they suffered. The campaign exposed many of the flaws of the Italian military for the first time, and showed that no matter how brave an individual soldier may be, the Fascist regime was incapable of waging war efficiently. Rather, what the brief campaign did achieve was to give Mussolini what he required - war casualties! He had earlier told Marshal Badoglio, his Chief of Staff, "I need only a few thousand dead to ensure I have the right to sit at the peace table in the capacity of a belligerent". The sacrifice of Italian soldiers did gain Mussolini a few alpine villages and occupation rights over the southern French province of Provence.

Mussolini's next military venture in the European theater was Italy's invasion of Greece four months later. Germany's virtual takeover of Romania without consulting the Italian dictator infuriated Mussolini, who decided to pay Hitler back "in his own coin". He looked around for a suitable victim and decided Greece would be perfect in the role of sacrificial lamb. Italian propaganda claimed the Greeks had no stomach to fight for a corrupt government that would capitulate and accept the invaders as rulers. The Italian invasion of Greece in late October 1940 was one of the worst-conceived and poorly planned campaigns of WWII. At the behest of Mussolini it was organized in less than two weeks by Italian generals who knew the army was not prepared for the invasion and who had little confidence in the outcome. It was not just his German ally that Mussolini kept in the dark about the invasion, as Marshal Graziani, Italian commander in North Africa and Chief of Army Staff, only heard about the invasion from a radio broadcast!

The invasion was launched from newly conquered Albania, which had only been part of the "Italian Empire" since April 1939. Just before the attack there were only about 140,000 Italian troops in Albania, and many of these were second-line units such as Carabinieri and Frontier Troops. In the few months before the invasion, a total of 60,000 more experienced troops had been sent back to Italy to help with the harvest as part of a 600,000-man demobilization designed to save money. This meant the majority of troops in the invasion force were inexperienced raw recruits. To make matters worse, the invading army was bulked out with Albanian volunteers who were almost totally unreliable.

The invasion force was made up of nine divisions of the 9th and 11th Armies, a total of 87,000 men, and 686 guns. Desperately lacking in motor transport, the Italians had only five days' worth of small-arms ammunition, 70 days of fuel for its few motor vehicles, and 40 days of other supplies. Another factor counting against the Italian invasion was that they were attacking along 240km of mountainous border (a third of the Albanian-Greek border is composed of high mountains). Incredibly, no maps had been prepared for these mountainous regions so troops were often advancing blindly into Greek territory. The weather was also against the Italians as the attack coincided with the Greek rainy season when rivers were swollen and temperatures dropped to below freezing. Most Italian soldiers did not have winter boots and this resulted in 13,000 cases of frostbite by the end of December.

It was also assumed the Italians had an overwhelming superiority in numbers and equipment over the Greeks, though this was not the case. In fact the Greeks had three regiments of infantry per division as opposed to Italy's two, plus it had more medium artillery and machineguns. Where the Italians did hold an advantage was in airpower and armor, with Greece having only a small air force and virtually no tanks. These two advantages were nullified by the fact that the air force was never employed during the early stages because of the weather, plus the terrain made the use of armored units difficult.

General Sebastiano Visconti-Prasca, the Italian commander in Albania, left a small covering force on his eastern flank in the Pindus Mountains and sent 70,000 men into Greece on 28 October. The Italians advanced in a four-pronged attack up to 40km into Greek territory, with the 11,000-strong *Julia* Alpini Division making good progress, even though by 31 October its men had been reduced to hard rations. After a few days of relatively easy progress,

Italian troops began facing frequent ambushes from overlooking mountains. In addition, they faced other obstacles such as destroyed bridges and seasonally swollen rivers.

The Greeks then launched a counteroffensive with three divisions, pushing the Italians back northwards. The *Julia* Alpini Division was surrounded by 8 November, forcing it into a disorderly retreat. By 14 November the Italians were in general retreat all along the front, and by the 18th heavy fighting was taking place at Koritsa just inside Greece. On 21 November the Greeks recaptured Koritsa, taking 2000 prisoners as well as 135 field guns and 600 machineguns. By 3 December the Greeks had crossed the Kalamas River and were advancing along the coast deep into Albanian territory. In a state of panic, Italy was meanwhile bringing in large numbers of piecemeal reinforcements through the northern Albanian ports they held. By 5 December they had established a defensive line running eastwards from Klimura on the coast. For the rest of the month, a stalemate ensued with both sides exhausted and generally holding what they had until the end of the year. Both sides suffered greatly from the cold during the winter months because uniforms were totally inadequate for the conditions. Uniforms soon became tatty and boots wore out, causing many soldiers on both sides to wrap their feet in rags. Due to no change of uniform, and sleeping in the open in often waterlogged trenches, the number of casualties from various afflictions such as dry gangrene rose alarmingly.

1941 opened with a major 13-division Greek attack launched on 4 January against the 16 Italian divisions now receiving further reinforcements. These reinforcements often arrived at the front in incomplete units with much of their heavy equipment, and even the soldiers' personal gear, missing. By January the number of Italian troops in Albania looked impressive, at least in theory, with 271,463 men being formed into a defensive wall to hold back further Greek advances. By 7 January the Greeks were advancing on the town of Klisura, with the town falling on the 10th. During this bitter fighting, both sides suffered heavy losses as they fought themselves to a standstill. The *Lupi di Toscana* and *Pinerolo* Infantry Divisions, and what remained of the *Julia* Alpini Division, suffered particularly heavy casualties in this fighting that lasted until the end of January. An Italian offensive to recapture Klisura on the 26th failed, and the fighting developed once again into a stalemate with neither side able to strike a decisive blow.

Mussolini decided to try and bring his authority to bear on the situation and arrived in Albania on 2 March for an inspection tour of the front ahead of a large-scale Italian spring offensive. This "Prima Verra" spring offensive began on 9 March and was intended to retake Klisura and give the Italians some face-saving victories before an expected military intervention by Germany. The offensive was undertaken by 17 Italian divisions (32 regiments) facing 13 Greek divisions (34 regiments) – it made initial gains before stalling on the 14th. Desperate frontal attacks on dug-in Greek positions cost the Italians dearly without gaining any real territory. More localized offensives continued after a brief respite, but again the Italians made little progress despite the suicidal bravery of some of their attacks. For the rest of March the fighting bogged down into a series of local attacks and counterattacks without any significant gains for either side.

Meanwhile, the British Expeditionary Force, W-Force, sent to aid the Greeks began disembarking on 7 March. This scratch four-division force of 58,000 British, New Zealand, Australian, and Free Polish troops was a mixture of North African veterans and raw recruits. Military aid had already been sent by Britain to Greece (this ironically included Italian artillery captured in Libya in 1940-41, as well as other armaments such as Universal Carriers) to form an ad hoc Greek armored brigade. The British force was poorly equipped with old, worn-out tanks, artillery and other equipment collected from various sources. Although sent to bolster the Greek war effort, the British Expeditionary Force could do little when faced with the intervention of Germany in April 1941.

The situation in Greece changed dramatically with the launch of Operation Marita by Germany at the start of April. Hitler's intervention in the Balkans had two motives - firstly to help his Italian ally finish off Greece, and secondly and more importantly, to punish Yugoslavia. Also, by occupying both countries he would remove any threat to his flank when he launched his

invasion of the Soviet Union, Operation Barbarossa, a few months later. Earlier, the Kingdom of Yugoslavia under the rule of its regent, Prince Paul, had agreed after a combination of German threats and promises to join the Tripartite Pact with Germany, Italy and Japan. Although Prince Paul was reluctant to throw in his lot with the Axis powers, he knew there was little choice for his isolated country. The agreement was signed on 25 March, but two days later a military coup by the pro-Allied Yugoslav military completely changed things. Hitler was outraged at this perceived betrayal by Yugoslavia and he immediately ordered the invasion of both Greece and Yugoslavia under the codename Operation Marita.

This Blitzkrieg campaign lasted from 6-27 April and resulted in the complete defeat and occupation of both Greece and Yugoslavia. During the German invasion, the Italian 9th Army in Albania advanced back into Greece making major inroads into Epirus by the 17th. On 21 April the major Greek armies surrendered to the Germans, but at Mussolini's insistence, the ceremony had to be repeated on the 23rd in front of an Italian representative. A total of 16 Greek divisions laid down their arms under these surrender terms, but other units continued to fight alongside British troops who waged a fighting retreat south through the Greek mainland. The British W-Force was eventually evacuated from ports in the south to the Greek island of Crete, which was duly captured by German forces at the beginning of June. With the fall of Crete, the conquest of Greece was complete and years of Axis occupation were to follow, with the Italian Army given the main garrison role until the fall of Mussolini in 1943.

Italy declared war on Yugoslavia on 6 April and the 2nd Army began attacking across the Italian-Yugoslav border on the 7th. The 2nd Army comprising the 5th, 6th and 11th Corps with eight infantry divisions, as well as the Celere Corps and Auto Transportable Corps, advanced along two axes. One force made for Llubjiana in Slovenia, which soon fell, while the other force advanced southwards along the Dalmatian coast. The Italians took several coastal towns including Zara, Sibenik, Split, and then finally Dubrovnik on the 17th. At the same time, the 9th Army invaded northwards from Albania with seven infantry divisions, one armored division, three cavalry regiments and two *Raggruppamento* of Blackshirt militiamen. This force also made for Dubrovnik. Western Montenegro and its southern coastline were taken by the 9th Army before they joined up with their comrades in the 2nd Army in Dubrovnik on 17 April. The Yugoslav Army surrendered the same day and 334,000 prisoners of war were taken. In their haste, however, the Germans and Italians let many Yugoslav soldiers demobilize and released others soon after. Many of these defeated men then took to the hills to continue the fight against the Axis as guerrillas.

Apart from the 8th Army on the Russian Front (see below), the main contribution of the Italian Army to the Axis war effort in Europe after April 1941 was as occupation garrisons. Large numbers of Italian troops were tied down in occupation roles in Greece and regions of Yugoslavia. Three Italian armies were given occupation duties - the 9th Army in Albania, Montenegro and Herzegovina, the 2nd Army in coastal Croatia and parts of Slovenia, and the 11th Army on the Greek mainland and scattered around various Greek islands. By early 1943 there were a total of 30 divisions committed to occupation duties in the Balkans, with six in Albania, nine in Greece and 15 in various regions of Yugoslavia. As well as regular troops, from 1941 Italian occupying authorities also raised local volunteers willing to fight against pro-communist partisans in parts of Yugoslavia. These were known as the Milizia Volontaria Anti-Communista (MVAC). MVAC units were formed in occupied regions of the country as well as in Italian-annexed areas such as Dalmatia, Slovenia and Montenegro. This extremely diverse organization included Catholic Slovenians and Dalmatians, as well as Greek Orthodox and Muslim volunteers. Altogether, almost 30,000 MVAC volunteers served in 119 detachments assigned to Italian divisions serving in their regions.

Large numbers of Italian troops were involved in various anti-partisan offensives in Yugoslavia during the occupation, fighting alongside German and local anti-communist volunteers. They suffered heavy casualties throughout the years of occupation, and in fact, more Italians were killed in Yugoslavia than in the North African campaign.

In the early hours of 22 June 1941, a few months after the end of fighting in the Balkans, Germany launched Operation Barbarossa, the invasion of the Soviet Union. Hitler only informed Mussolini of the invasion as it began, and although the Duce took this lack of a pre-warning as a slight, he immediately offered substantial numbers of troops to fight in the anti-communist crusade against Fascism's archenemy. As in June 1940, Mussolini wanted to share in any spoils from the expected defeat of the Soviet Union, so he was in a rush to get his troops to the front. He shared Hitler's views on the racial inferiority of Russian people and he fully expected the German Army - with his help - would make short work of the Soviet Armed Forces. The offer of an Italian expeditionary force to fight in Russia was not greeted with enthusiasm by Hitler, but Mussolini's insistence meant he could not really refuse his ally's help. Hitler would have much preferred the Italians to concentrate their efforts on the fighting in North Africa. A 62,000-man Corpo Spedizione Italiane in Russia (CSIR) was quickly organized. It consisted of two infantry divisions, the *Torino*, *Pasubio* and 3rd Light Celere Divisions. With only eight antitank guns and eight light antiaircraft guns per division, plus a few batteries of field artillery, the CSIR was poorly armed for the fighting it was to face there. Initial armor consisted of a few L3 light tanks that had proved totally obsolescent in the fighting in Libya in 1940.

The CSIR arrived at the front after a 25-day journey from Italy to the southern Ukraine, including disembarkation at railheads in Romania. In total, 225 trains were used to transport the CSIR to Romania, from where the Italians then had to travel another 300km to their concentration areas. Finally arriving at the front in August 1941, they immediately fought a long-running engagement known by the Italians as the Battle of Two Rivers (the Bug and Dnieper). The advance to the Dnieper River was led by the *Pasubio* Infantry Division using most of the *Torino* Division's motor transport. In September the *Torino* Division fighting alongside the German SS Wiking Division took the town of Dnepropetrovsk, thereby gaining the praise of the German commander. In the advance on the industrial region of the Donets Basin in October, the CSIR covered the left flank of the 11th Army (part of the German Army Group South) as the first snows of the Russian winter fell.

Through October and November, the CSIR advanced through the Donets Basin taking little-known but strategic towns such as Jekatervina, Gorlovka and Skotowatoya, and in the process taking 12,000 Soviet prisoners. With the conquest of the Donets Basin, Army Group South moved towards the city of Rostov again with the CSIR on its left flank. Although Rostov fell to the Germans, Soviet resistance was growing and the Italians and their German ally had to go onto the defensive for the winter as temperatures dropped as low as -30°C. As in France in 1940 and Greece/Albania in 1940-41, ordinary Italian soldiers suffered terribly in the conditions with little or no winter clothing available. They were not alone in this as the Russian winter also took the German Army by surprise, their soldiers inadequately clothed for the extremely cold temperatures.

During the Christmas period, heavy Soviet attacks against Italian defenses cost the CSIR 1,347 dead in one week. The Soviet attacks had exposed many weaknesses in the CSIR, not only in their arms and equipment, but also in the men who were worn out and in need of replacement. On 21 January 1942, a major Soviet offensive was launched that continued into February and March, with Italian and German troops forming ad hoc forces to counter these attacks. Limited reinforcements did begin arriving at this time from Italy, but although these included the elite *Monte Cervino* Alpini Ski Battalion and a Croatian legion, they were not enough to make a major difference. At least the CSIR survived the winter, and by May 1942, Axis forces were preparing to go over to the offensive again. As before, the CSIR was to protect the flank of the German III Corps as it advanced towards its primary objective of the Crimea. After initial resistance, advancing Axis forces took 200,000+ prisoners in ten days and made good progress. At this juncture, Mussolini decided to drastically increase the Italian commitment to the Eastern Front.

Mussolini was adamant the number of Italians fighting in Russia should be larger than contingents from Romania, Hungary or any other ally of Germany. He called the CSIR commander, General Messe, to a conference where he suggested the Italian contingent should be substantially increased in size. Messe was totally against the expansion of the CSIR into a much larger force and was dismissed from his command because of it. In July 1942, against the advice of Messe and other senior officers, the CSIR was increased in size to a ten-division formation named the 8th Army, or *Armata Italiana in Russia* (ARMIR). By Italian standards the ARMIR was well supplied with motor vehicles and artillery. With seven new divisions added to the three already in Russia, the increase in numbers of men and equipment was a major commitment Italy could ill afford.

The new divisions were the *Sforzesca*, *Ravenna*, *Cosseria* and *Vicenza* Infantry Divisions, as well as the *Tridentina*, *Julia* and *Cuneense* Alpini Divisions. The 8th Army also included two German divisions (298th and 62nd), a Croatian volunteer legion, and three legions of MVSN volunteers. With a strength of 235,000 men, 1000 artillery pieces, 420 mortars, 25,000 horses, 16,700 motor vehicles and 64 aircraft, the 8th Army was a major commitment on the part of Mussolini. The motor vehicles in particular would have been better employed in North Africa where even a fraction of them could have given static Italian forces the mobility that is so vital in desert fighting. Even though the resources that Italy put into the Russian Front were a mammoth effort on their part, they were only a tiny proportion of what was needed to sustain the kind of total warfare fought in the East.

Now under the command of General Italo Garibaldi, Messe's replacement, the 8th Army continued in the same role as the CSIR and advanced with the Germans towards the River Don. From August 1942, a series of defensive battles were fought by the 8th Army along the line of the Don as the Soviets built up their strength for a major offensive. At the same time, to the southeast of Italian positions on the Don, the titanic battle for the city of Stalingrad was taking place. The attacking German 6th Army (with a strength of 284,000 men) was eventually cut off in a salient by a Soviet offensive that destroyed Romanian divisions guarding the flanks. Completely surrounded, the Germans struggled on until 31 January 1943 when 90,000 surviving men of the 6th Army surrendered.

Earlier Soviet offensives had thrown the Germans and Italians back from their lines along the Don. On 16 December after a 90-minute artillery barrage, the Soviet 1st Guards and 6th Armies broke through the 8th Army's left flank and advanced 65km. Then the Soviet 3rd Guards Army (made up of four tank corps and one mechanized corps) attacked the 8th Army's right flank. Totally outgunned, the Italians were forced to retreat across the open steppes, leaving 15,000 men cut off and surrounded. As the 8th Army fled it disintegrated and although many of its men reached new German defensive lines, it was finished as a useful military force. It was decided to withdraw the 8th Army from Russia, and by the end of March 1943 the majority of these Italians were back home. Some Italian units did continue to serve in the anti-partisan role in Russia until the fall of Mussolini, but the impending Allied threat to Italy itself meant as many men as possible were needed at home.

The losses of Mussolini's adventure in Russia were terrible for Italy, with almost 85,000 killed or missing, and 30,000 wounded. Although human losses were tragic, losses in material were in some ways more catastrophic for the Italian war effort, with 18,000 motor vehicles and 820 artillery pieces lost. These figures are small compared with the scale of fighting on the Russian Front, but for Italy with its limited industrial capacity, losses in equipment were irreplaceable. When the Allies invaded Sicily in July 1943, they faced second-line, badly equipped units that could have done with a portion of the weaponry lost in Russia.

Acknowledgements
I must thank the following contributors for kindly allowing me to use photographs from their collections: James Burd, Dino Di Mascio, Joe Granata, Alexei Ivanov, Marco Novarese, Nicola Pignato, Alejandro M. de Quesada, Lino Scafiano, Robert Stedman, Rex Tyre, Count Ernesto Vitetti and the staff of the National Museum of Contemporary History, Llubjiana, and of the Ufficio Storico Dello Stato Maggiore Escercito. Particular thanks to Filippo Cappellano, who provided me with the majority of photographs for this book.

The Italian Army Pre-1940

A motorized unit of the Italian Army photographed on 22 October 1940. The massed ranks of motor vehicles and artillery gives an initial impression of the armed might of Mussolini's mechanized army. The photograph also illustrates, however, one of the fundamental weaknesses of the Italian Army – the unit possesses WWI-vintage field guns. Nearly all of Italy's artillery pieces were out of date and many were booty taken in war reparations from the Austro-Hungarians in 1918.

As with the previous photograph, this image of row after row of *Carro Veloce* L35 tankettes is meant to impress the viewer with the sheer number of tanks on parade. In 1940 the Italian Army did have more than 1000 in service in various models, but they were too lightly armored and poorly armed to be of any real combat use. Nevertheless, they did see service on all fronts including Russia from 1941 onwards, though they were soon relegated to light escort duties as soon as heavier tanks became available.

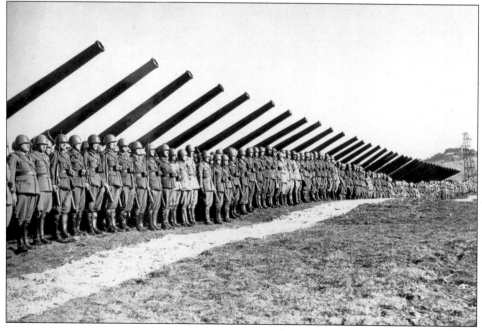

In another illustration of Italy's ill-preparedness in fighting a modern war, this heavy artillery regiment poses just before the war with its 149/35 howitzers forming a canopy over the crews. The 149/35 was one of the oldest Italian artillery pieces in service, the design dating from 1900. This antiquated gun should have been replaced by the modern 149/40 but this model was never produced in enough quantity, meaning there were still nearly 900 149/35 guns in service in June 1940. Large numbers of the 149/35 served on the Greek-Albanian Front in 1940-41 and in North Africa until 1942.

In a nicely posed photograph, this smartly turned out 47mm antitank gun crew takes up position around the weapon during a pre-war exercise. If this scene had been in a real combat situation, the men would have been extremely exposed and vulnerable to enemy fire. The men have taken the wheels off the carriage to give it more stability and the firer aims through the sights while adjusting the trajectory with the wheel on the left.

A Fucile Mitriagliatori Breda Modello 30 light machinegun crew on field exercises fires their weapon from the cover of tall grass. The Breda 30, as it was known, was a development of the Model 1924. It was certainly not one of the best-designed machineguns in service during WWII, but it was all the Italians had. Each infantry regiment in 1940 had 117 Bredas, as well as 27 of either of the two main types of heavy machinegun.

During the buildup to Italy's entry into the war, this Fiat 1914/35 medium machinegun crew trains with their weapon. The 1914/35 was a modification of the Revelli Modello 1914, which was the standard Italian heavy machinegun of WWI. Commonly called the "Fiat-Revelli" because it was manufactured by the former, it was by most accounts worse than the original version that had a water-cooled barrel. Its faults included a barrel that overheated and an oiled lubrication system that easily gritted up in service.

The loader of a mortar crew drops a round into the tube of his 81mm 81/14 Modello 35 before Italy's declaration of war against Britain and France. The photograph can be dated before 1940 by the corporal's chevron rank insignia, which is the type used from 1937 to 1940. Before 1937, the chevrons pointed upwards and this NCO looks like he has taken the old curved insignia and turned it upside down to adapt it to the new dress regulations.

In this photograph taken on the French border before the war, a group of officers from various units leave their headquarters during an exercise. The identifiable officers are from left to right, a lieutenant colonel, and in the center of the three man group, a major of transport troops with an Alpini colonel next to him (with the divisional shield on his left sleeve). The next officer in the foreground is the general of a division, and finally the man on the far right is an Alpini lieutenant colonel.

Western Alpine Front, June 1940

Wireless operators of the artillery branch are using an RF2 radio on the Alpine Front in 1940. The crew has set up their communication post in a disputed village on the Italian-French border. RF2 radios were used mainly for communications between artillery units and divisional headquarters. Too heavy for one man, the RF2 was usually carried by pack mule, or when necessary, by its two-man crew over short distances.

Artillerymen of the Guardia alla Frontiera (Frontier Guard) stand in front of a Skoda 380/15 howitzer on the border with France in 1940. The Italian Frontier Guard was not only responsible for patrolling Italy's borders, but they were also heavily involved in military operations alongside the regular army. During the invasion of France in June 1940, there were ten Frontier artillery groups and eight Frontier Guard infantry units on the strength of the invading 1st and 4th Italian Armies. This 380mm 380/15 artillery piece was the second heaviest gun in the Italian Army, but there were only five in service in 1940.

A fully equipped Alpino - weighed down by his equipment and with a Carcano M1891 rifle slung over his shoulder - advances past a rocky outcrop. Alpini equipment included a mountain rucksack, climbing rope, axe and an M1934-issue alpenstock useful for traversing the mountainous terrain typical of the campaign against France in 1940.

Artillerymen of an Alpini division prepare to load up their mules with equipment before moving forward. An Alpini division included an artillery regiment with its pack artillery easily broken down into several loads that could be carried by mule. With previous experience of fighting along their mountainous borders, the Italians made widespread use of these hardy creatures during WWII on several fronts.

Camouflaged SPA 38 light trucks drive through a border village and receive an enthusiastic welcome from some of the locals. As with most border conflicts many of the people of Italian ancestry in the mixed Italian-French populations would greet the invaders as "liberators".

Pavesi Model 30-A artillery tractors pulling 105/28 Ansaldo-Schneider guns halt on a mountain road to await further orders before moving forward. Pavesi artillery tractors were introduced into Italian service in the early 1930s and came in three main models; there were more than 2000 in service in 1940. Pavesi tractors came into their own in the muddy conditions faced on the Greek and Russian Fronts. Only about 50% of Italian troops actually reached the frontline before the end of fighting on 24 June.

Camouflaged SPA TL37 light artillery tractors towing ammunition trailers stop along a rain-drenched mountain road. The TL37 was an excellent vehicle that carried a six-man gun crew and towed either a 75mm or 100mm field gun at speeds of up to 40km/h. Because of the speed of this vehicle, older wooden-wheeled field guns had to be modernized and fitted with metal wheels with rubber tires. By June 1940 this process was still in its early stages with 467 75mm field guns and 100 100mm types adapted.

An 81mm 81/14 Model 35 mortar team carries their weapon across hilly terrain as they advance towards French positions on the Alpine Front. The 81mm mortar is broken up into its three component parts with the barrel carried by one crewman, the base-plate by another, and the legs by a third man. A fourth man carries a spare barrel, and the fifth man presumably carries a few rounds as well as other kit.

A column of Benelli 500 M36 motor-tricycles stops for a break as they advance into French territory along a road at the base of the Alps. Benelli motor-tricycles were useful little vehicles widely employed by the Italians on all fronts during the war. The lead motorcyclist is dressed in conventional infantry fashion but has a pair of riding boots on. A Carcano carbine is slung over his shoulder.

A pair of 75mm 75/27 Model 11 field guns is brought into action to bombard French positions from a hillside. Artillery of this caliber would make little impression on some of the strongly protected French fortifications during the short campaign. The fact that Mussolini only gave his generals a few days' notice to launch an offensive against France meant that the heavy artillery needed to bombard their positions was not in place.

A Bersaglieri unit in the Mont Cenis sector unloads bicycles from the back of four Bianchi Mediolanum 36 trucks. Bicycle-mounted Bersaglieri would be transported near to the front in trucks before continuing their advance. The French campaign was a series of stop-start advances, and in the Mont Cenis sector, the Italian advance was stopped by the French Turra emplacement with its two 75mm field guns.

The crew of a 75/27 M1911 field gun gets ready to shell French fortifications in the distant hills. While the NCO appears to be reading instructions from his manual, his men wait patiently to load their gun. The 75/27 was one of the most important Italian field guns in terms of numbers, with more than 1800 in service in 1940.

An anti-vehicle obstacle is wheeled out of its holding shed on the Italian-French border to block the road. Both the Italians and the French had well-constructed fortifications on their borders, and any unsupported infantry assault against them was bound to cause heavy casualties for the attacking force.

A column of Autocarrette OM 36MT light trucks halts their advance through an alpine village. The Autocarrette came in several models and was designed to traverse difficult and especially mountainous terrain. During the French campaign, they were mainly used by the *Trieste* Motorized Division.

A mixed group of artillerymen and Fascist PNF officials poses for the camera the day after the French bombardment of the Italian border town of Ventimiglia. All the soldiers wear the bustina side cap, and some have the leather gaiters and two-pocket leather bandolier worn by the artillery.

This destroyed L3-35 light tank lying on the side of a mountain road looks as though it has been opened by a can opener after being hit by French shellfire. The four battalions of L3-35 tanks used during the campaign suffered heavy casualties either from French mines or artillery fire. The 1st Battalion was sent against French positions on 23 June, and the 4th Battalion did the same the following day. On both occasions these units suffered losses to French minefields. (Tank Museum)

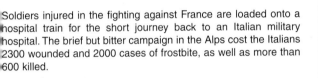

Soldiers injured in the fighting against France are loaded onto a hospital train for the short journey back to an Italian military hospital. The brief but bitter campaign in the Alps cost the Italians 2300 wounded and 2000 cases of frostbite, as well as more than 600 killed.

After the cessation of hostilities on the French-Italian border, Italian Carabinieri parade in front of a French gendarmerie barracks, the new HQ of the local Frontier brigade. The soldiers display the black cloth collar of the M1937 tunic, which was replaced during the early stages of the war by a gray-green one.

13

Greek-Albanian Front, 1940-41

Italian soldiers march confidently into Greece at the start of the invasion in late October 1940. On the surface their commanders were confident in Visconti Prasca, the Italian commander, saying that morale was "very high". Prasca expressed the concern that the Epirus region should be captured quickly before the start of the rainy season. The initial early gains against Greek forces that strategically withdrew in front of them led the Italians into a false sense of optimism. When the Greeks were ready, they struck and destroyed large numbers of Italian units, beginning to push them back into Albania.

Alpini artillerymen disembark at an Albanian port carrying as much of their gear as they can down the ship's gangplank. The Albanian ports of Durazzo and Valona were inadequate for bringing in the sheer amount of men and material the invasion of Greece required. Throughout most of the campaign in Greece, the situation at the ports was chaotic and disorganized, a situation not helped by the small capacity of these harbors.

Italian Alpini and artillery move in a long straggling column along a mountain road on the Albanian-Greek Front. The artillery is being towed by Pavesi P4-100 4x4 artillery tractors manufactured for the Italian Army from 1936-42. At the front of the column are two mules carrying between them the barrel and carriage of a 65mm M17 mountain gun. Although the elderly 65mm gun was being replaced at the start of the war, there were still 700 of them in service in 1940.

During the bitter fighting of early November, an Alpini column advances into Greece with the unit's transport mules. In the foreground, heavily laden foot soldiers begin to climb into the foothills in an attempt to take the high ground from the Greeks. No two soldiers appear to have the same kit and one of them has fastened a leather suitcase containing his personal belongings to his back.

Artillerymen manhandle a 2470kg 105/28 field gun into position during fighting on the Greek Front in November 1940. The 105/28 was a reliable gun that served the Italian Army well in WWI, having entered service in 1914. It then went on to serve on every front during WWII, although by 1943 many were being used as coastal artillery. The 105/28 was modernized by fitting rubber-tired wheels but only 108 of the 839 in service in 1942 had been converted in this way. In the fighting against Greece, both sides were evenly matched in artillery with both nations' divisions having nine batteries each.

A draught mule is stuck in mud on the Greek-Albanian Front while its hapless handler looks on in despair. The invasion of Greece coincided with the start of the rainy season, and conditions like these were encountered until the ground froze, which brought problems of its own. Both Italian and Greek soldiers were poorly equipped for the harsh conditions they faced in the winter of 1940. Italian hobnailed boots failed to protect soldiers from the frostbite that caused heavy casualties on both sides.

With a helping push from some of their infantry comrades, Bersaglieri motorcyclists struggle to make progress along a deeply rutted and mud-covered track in the Kalamas sector of the Greek Front in 1941. Conditions like these made any advance through the mountainous terrain of Greece extremely difficult.

Bersaglieri motorcyclists on their Moto Guzzi Alce 500cc machines slither and slide as they try and advance across a riverbed in early 1941. The Alce could reach speeds of 90km/h and the Bersaglieri were trained to exploit their machines' performance to scout ahead. However, conditions in Albania and Greece made any kind of progress very difficult, and the motorcyclists, like other Italian mechanized elements, were soon bogged down. Greek rivers were swollen with rain and many were virtually impassable.

In a photograph dated 10 February 1941, artillerymen drag their 75/37 Model 06 field gun through the snow. As the Italian Army became bogged down on the Albanian Front, much of the world's press ridiculed their failure to defeat Greece. The original U.S. caption to this photo stated the Italians "move backwards in Greece".

Italian Fiat 665 5-ton trucks struggle through a blizzard on the Greek-Albanian Front after the road had just been opened for them. The severe 1940-41 winter faced by both the Italian and Greek Armies made getting supplies up to the frontline a constant problem. Fiat 3-ton, 5-ton and 6-ton trucks were workhorses for much of the Italian Army, plus they were also used by the Wehrmacht.

As an Alpini ski trooper looks on, an infantry patrol moves up a snow-covered hillside in the Pindos region of the Albanian Front. This Alpino armed with a Carcano carbine is well equipped with a snow camouflage suit over his gray-green uniform, and he has an Alpini rucksack on his back. His infantry comrades are struggling up the slope with full kit and are armed with the more cumbersome Carcano M1891 rifle.

With its wheels clogged with mud from the Albanian winter, a 75/18 Model 1934 howitzer of an Alpini division's artillery has been dragged into position on a hillside. The 75/18 was produced by Ansaldo and was one of the more modern Italian artillery pieces in WWII.

17

Alpini relax and play a game of cards during a lull in fighting on the Greek-Albanian Front in 1941. Life for the ordinary Italian soldier in the winter of 1940-41 was pretty bleak and conditions were often terrible. The Fascist Party collected warm clothing and gifts for troops, as well as setting up rest areas in the rear to try and improve their morale.

A fallen Guastatori assault engineer lies beside his Breda-30 light machinegun after an Italian attack on Greek positions. The courage of the individual Italian soldier was never in doubt and many of the most fervent Fascists died with Mussolini's name on their lips. As was to be the case in most campaigns in WWII, the ordinary Italian soldier was let down by the regime's administrative weaknesses.

Mussolini peers through a field telescope during a visit to XXV Army Corps of the 9th Army on the Greek Front in early 1941, as Italy prepared for a big "Prima verra" spring offensive. He is surrounded by attentive staff officers, including General Biroli at Mussolini's right shoulder, second-in-command of the 9th Army. In the same group, although not visible here, are General Cavallero, the Army Chief of Staff, and divisional generals of Alpini and infantry, as well as high-ranking officers of the MVSN militia. The Duce wears the uniform of Field Marshal of the Empire, a rank held only by Mussolini and King Victor Emanuel III.

During the same inspection tour of the Greek-Albanian Front in early 1941, Il Duce inspects a motorcycle unit whose commander is returning Mussolini's salute. The unit is equipped with Moto Guzzi motorcycles and a single motor-tricycle carrying the unit's radio in its cargo compartment. Behind the motor-tricycle stands the two-man crew that operates the unit's radio. All the men wear the motorcyclists' version of the leather crash helmet; this was in brown leather whereas the tankers' version was black.

The crew of an M13/40 medium tank of the 134th *Centauro* Armored Division lines up for an inspection on the Greek-Albanian Front. At the start of the invasion of Greece in October 1940, *Centauro* was equipped with L33-35 tankettes, before being reinforced in November 1940 by a 37-tank battalion of the much better M13/40. M13/40s serving in Greece were finished in a plain gray-green camouflage.

An artilleryman reads a letter from home while resting near the frontline in Greece during the 1940-41 fighting. His helmet decal, lacking a unit numeral in the center, indicates he is from divisional artillery. Like many Italian soldiers during the early part of the war, he still wears the M1937 black velvet collar on his tunic.

This mortar team fires its 81mm 81/14 Model 35 weapon in support of an attack during fighting on the Albanian-Greek Front. Each infantry division had a mortar battalion with 12 81mm mortars, as well as a mortar company in each of the division's two regiments (with six mortars per unit). The Model 35 mortar was based, as were most types in use with combatants, on the French Brandt.

The crew of a Skoda 100mm 100/17 Model 1916 howitzer sights their weapon during fighting in Greece in 1941. This photograph gives an impression of the type of terrain the Italian Army faced, with mountains towering above their gun position. 100/17 howitzers were taken in large numbers as war reparations from the defeated Austro-Hungarians in 1918, and were used as divisional artillery by the Italians. The gun could be broken down into three parts for transport over difficult terrain by cart, but it was rather heavy for this purpose.

An L3-35 tank commander pauses to pose for the camera on the Greek-Albanian Front. These small and virtually useless tankettes made up the majority of Italian armored vehicles in Greece. The Greeks, however, only had a handful of tanks to oppose the Italians, though they did capture a large number of L3s. Mountainous terrain meant armor did not play a part in the bitter 1940-41 fighting, and the arrival of extra armor in the spring made little difference to the campaign.

An M13/40 crewman climbs out of the side hatch of his medium tank on the Greek Front in March 1941. He wears a standard-issue black leather tankers' helmet and coat over blue overalls. Italian tanks faced little real opposition from the tiny Greek armored branch during the invasion, as they had only a handful of obsolete French light tanks and two British 6-tonners. The Greeks had ordered 14 more tanks before the war but these failed to arrive before the invasion.

Footsore Alpini of the *Verona* Battalion of the *Tridentina* Division march along the bottom of a valley during an advance in Albania in March 1941. They are carrying all their kit on their backs and several of the men have rain capes slung over their shoulders. The man in the rear has an M1909 wool cape. Soldiers advancing like this along a valley floor were extremely vulnerable to Greeks on the high ground above them.

A column of reinforcements for the Albanian Front marches forwards as Italy tries to push Greek forces back into their own country. The shortage of motor transport means these men will have to trudge for miles before they reach the fighting. Mules were useful on the Albanian Front where roads were often unsuitable for trucks and other motor vehicles.

As the ascent into the mountains begins, the column starts to straggle and men carry their rifles and kit in whatever way is most comfortable. The officer in the center of the column with his much smarter uniform shows that even higher ranks had to walk. The lack of motor transport was supposedly compensated for by Italian soldiers' ability to march 40km in one day and 160km over five days.

A Breda 20mm 20/65 M35 antiaircraft gun crew swings their gun into the vertical position as they fire at attacking Greek aircraft. The three-man crew of the Breda was trained to use their weapon against ground targets as well as in its main role as a light antiaircraft gun. As the Breda was fed by 12-round ammunition clips, the crew had to be expert to maintain steady automatic fire by fitting fresh magazines as they ran out.

A battery of four 152/37 152mm heavy guns fires at Greek positions during the Italian spring offensive. These former Austro-Hungarian guns were taken as war reparations in 1918 with 30 of the 44 guns produced going into Italian service. From March 1941, two batteries (131st and 132nd of the 51st Artillery Group) used them in Greece and then Yugoslavia.

Fully kitted out Blackshirt militiamen bound for the Greek Front board a troop train. The arrival of Blackshirt reinforcements caused a great deal of resentment from regular Italian soldiers who were angry their Fascist comrades had missed some of the bitterest fighting in the winter of 1940-41. At the same time, some ardent Fascist reinforcements were said to envy the veterans who proved themselves in the earlier fighting.

Other reinforcements for the Greek Front board a light plane at Puglia in Italy, as forces are built up for the spring offensive. Reinforcement of the Albanian Front was almost totally disorganized, with men arriving in incomplete units without proper equipment. They were then thrown piecemeal into the fighting, and consequently their morale suffered even before they saw action. (Filippo Cappellano)

Blackshirts of the 15th *Leonessa* Battalion, 1st Blackshirt Legion (attached to the Wolves of Tuscany *Lupi Di Toscana* 7th Infantry Division) share a cigarette. The division was sent to Albania in January 1941 and suffered heavy casualties before being withdrawn for occupation duties. Blackshirts were identifiable by the silver fasces badge worn on the collar and the same stenciled symbol worn on the M35 steel helmet.

A group of Alpini officers enjoy a break from fighting, with the officer on the right taking a drink from his canteen's metal cup. The officer on the left is wearing the lace-up white overalls jacket worn by some Alpini units.

An officer of the Finance Guard takes a smoke break outside his dugout in Albania during the spring of 1941. The Finance Guard was primarily responsible for anti-smuggling duties in the Italian Army, and in peacetime it came under the authority of the Ministry of Finance. They also had a combat role during wartime when they were under the command of the War Ministry. Along with other second-line units like the Frontier Guard and Frontier Militia, they were used as frontline border troops especially in the Balkans.

An artillery lieutenant in command of a forward command post checks the range of Greek positions. Italian divisional artillery on the Greek-Albanian Front, like those in the deserts of North Africa, performed well. This was despite the fact they were in most cases using out-of-date field guns in difficult terrain better suited to mountain artillery.

Watched by a curious group of Bersaglieri and infantry, two logistic support troops of the 9th Army Servizio Logistico operate a mobile steam sterilizing unit to clean uniforms and blankets to kill lice and other parasites. The Italian logistic network for frontline troops in Greece was hit and miss, with some divisions arriving at the front without their support services. This meant ordinary soldiers sometimes went hungry.

A Bersaglieri motorcyclist in the vanguard of Operation Marita looks curiously at a Greek road sign in April 1941. Much to Mussolini's annoyance, Greece signed an armistice with Germany on 21 April. In an attempt to placate his ally, Hitler ordered the ceremony be repeated two days later with the Italians present this time.

Raising their daggers in the air in a victory salute, jubilant Volunteer Militia for National Security (MVSN), more commonly called the Blackshirts or Camicia Nere (CCNN), gather on a hillside to celebrate victory over Greece. The Blackshirts surround their commanding officers who were often local Fascist Party officials with no real military training. Despite Mussolini's hope that the Blackshirts would become the elite force of the Italian military, most did not perform as well as their regular army comrades, largely due to a lack of training and their poor standard of officers. Every infantry division was supposed to have an MVSN legion made up of two battalions, each battalion having 650 men and 20 officers.

After the defeat of Greece, Mussolini - and on his right, Marshal Ugo Cavallero, the Supreme Commander of the Army, and General Ubaldu Soddu, Commander of the Army in Greece - inspects units in an Albanian town. Born in 1880, Cavallero began his military career at the Modena Military Academy before serving in the Italian-Turkish War of 1911-12 before reaching the rank of brigadier general by 1918. In 1940 he succeeded the "retired" Badoglio as supreme commander, having previously been Commander-in-Chief of Italian forces in East Africa.

Private, 2nd Tridentina Alpini Division Western Alps, 1940

During the brief but costly campaign on the mountainous Italian-French border in June 1940, four specially trained Alpini mountain divisions were involved in the fighting.

Alpini divisions were recruited from the mountainous provinces of Italy and gained a good reputation during WWII as some of the best troops in the Italian Army. The short Western Alps campaign did not really give the Alpini a chance to show their prowess, but they were heavily involved from 1940 onwards in every campaign in the European theater. They were especially heavily involved in the invasion of Greece in October 1940, and in the fighting in Russia in 1941-43.

This Alpini soldier does not have his full kit on and has discarded his M1939 alpine rucksack and M1934 alpenstock walking stick before he conducts an assault. His tunic is the pre-war M1937 model with black felt collar that was replaced during the early war years by the gray-green type. Underneath his tunic, this soldier wears a gray-green pullover instead of the standard gray-green shirt. Trousers are the pantaloon type tucked into a pair of ribbed heavy woolen socks worn with special mountain boots. The color of the pompom on the Alpini hat indicated which battalion he belonged to, with the soldiers of 1st Battalion having white, the 2nd red, the 3rd green, and the 4th blue. Besides his standard gray-green leather belt with twin ammunition pouches, his includes a canvas haversack and metal water bottle in its canvas holder.

ZGONNÍK '07

Captain, Firenze 41st Infantry Division Albania, 1941

This infantry captain consulting his notebook belongs to the *Firenze* Infantry Division, which was partially mobilized in June 1940 and sent to fight the French that month. After being brought up to full strength, the division was sent to Albania in March 1941 as part of the massive buildup of Italian units on the Greek-Albanian Front. In April the division was part of the Italian force invading Yugoslavia from Albania, and it captured the town of Bibar. It then became part of the occupying force in Montenegro before surrendering to Germans in September 1943. However, a large number of the division's men elected to join local partisans in Yugoslavia and over the border in Albania rather than capitulating to the Germans.

The captain wears an M1940 gray-green woolen cloth jacket with his division's tabs on its lapels, while his rank is shown by the gold braid backed in red insignia on its cuff. His *bustina* side cap is made from a lighter gray cloth than the jacket, and it has the infantry branch badge on the front. Under his jacket he wears a gray-green cotton shirt and tie, plus he has a pair of gabardine cloth breeches on with the infantry-branch red stripe down the outer leg. Boots are the standard black leather officer's type that could be purchased privately in a better quality if the wearer could afford it. On his Sam Brown belt he has a holster for his Beretta M1934 automatic pistol, the favorite sidearm of the Italian Army during the war.

ZGONNÍK'07

Motorcyclist, 5th Bersaglieri Regiment Centauro Armored Division Yugoslavia, 1941

Bersaglieri (sharpshooters) were formed in 1836 as the army's light infantry of the Italian state of Piedmont, which, after the unification of Italy in the 1860s, became the Royal Italian Army. By 1940 Bersaglieri regiments were attached to motorized and armored formations of the Italian Army as mobile infantry. They were usually mounted in trucks or motorcycles to keep up with the fast-moving formations they served in. This man belongs to the 5th Regiment attached to the *Centauro* Armored Division, this unit serving in Greece and Yugoslavia in 1940-41. During the campaign in Yugoslavia in April 1941, motorcyclists like this moved ahead of their formations as the Royal Yugoslav Army disintegrated before the invading Germans and Italians.

This man wears a special canvas pullover smock with laced front, a practical and popular uniform item worn throughout the war. On his left sleeve he has the specialist badge for a dispatch rider, while the gold chevrons indicate he is a sergeant. On his M1933 steel helmet he proudly wears the black cockerel feathers worn by the Bersaglieri since their establishment. Even though wearing this type of adornment on a steel helmet may seem a little archaic, the Bersaglieri would never go into action without them if they could possibly help it. Also on the front of his helmet is the stenciled branch badge of the Bersaglieri with the Roman numeral for "5" in the center. The rest of his uniform is made up of gray-green reinforced breeches and black boots worn with black leather gaiters to protect the lower leg when riding his motorcycle. His ammunition pouches are specific to the Bersaglieri and carry spare clips for his Carcano M1891 carbine.

ZGONNÍK

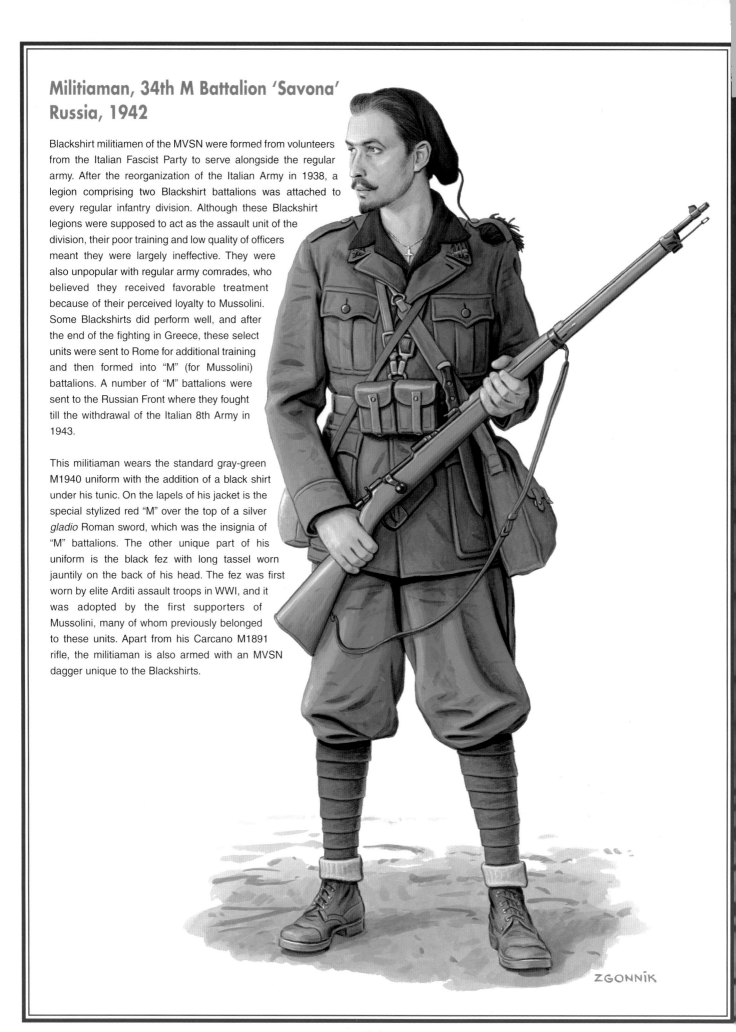

Militiaman, 34th M Battalion 'Savona' Russia, 1942

Blackshirt militiamen of the MVSN were formed from volunteers from the Italian Fascist Party to serve alongside the regular army. After the reorganization of the Italian Army in 1938, a legion comprising two Blackshirt battalions was attached to every regular infantry division. Although these Blackshirt legions were supposed to act as the assault unit of the division, their poor training and low quality of officers meant they were largely ineffective. They were also unpopular with regular army comrades, who believed they received favorable treatment because of their perceived loyalty to Mussolini. Some Blackshirts did perform well, and after the end of the fighting in Greece, these select units were sent to Rome for additional training and then formed into "M" (for Mussolini) battalions. A number of "M" battalions were sent to the Russian Front where they fought till the withdrawal of the Italian 8th Army in 1943.

This militiaman wears the standard gray-green M1940 uniform with the addition of a black shirt under his tunic. On the lapels of his jacket is the special stylized red "M" over the top of a silver *gladio* Roman sword, which was the insignia of "M" battalions. The other unique part of his uniform is the black fez with long tassel worn jauntily on the back of his head. The fez was first worn by elite Arditi assault troops in WWI, and it was adopted by the first supporters of Mussolini, many of whom previously belonged to these units. Apart from his Carcano M1891 rifle, the militiaman is also armed with an MVSN dagger unique to the Blackshirts.

ZGONNIK

Mussolini, Marshal Cavallero and General Soddu inspect a cavalry regiment at the close of fighting in Greece in April 1941. The invading Italian Army in October 1940 included three cavalry regiments, but there was little scope for the deployment of mounted troops in the early fighting. In the April fighting, however, cavalry played a greater role as the more mobile Italian and German Armies rolled back the Greeks and Yugoslavs.

Dagger-wielding Blackshirts of the *Bari* Infantry Division parade for the camera in Greece with their Legion *labaro* banner adorned with the imperial eagle. Each MVSN legion had its own *labaro* with its unit numeral followed by Legione at the top, and its name along the bottom, both in gold. The reverse side of the banner had the national flag and Italian coat of arms in the center, fringed in gold at the bottom.

Yugoslavia, 1941-43

A motorcyclist armed with a Breda 30 light machinegun mounted on his handlebars stops and waits for his comrades on the outskirts of Ljubljana at they advance through Slovenia on 12 April 1941. His machine is a Moto Guzzi MT17 solo on which he has piled a mixture of personal gear and other kit.

Sappers practice wire-cutting on the Yugoslav border just prior to the invasion of that country. With its 13 divisions, the 2nd Army was poised on the Italian-Yugoslav border, while the 9th Army with eight divisions was ready to invade from Italian-controlled northern Albania. Both armies had numerous attached units to reinforce regular divisions, including a large number of border and other second-line troops.

During the Italian advance into Slovenia in April 1941, a unit of Bersaglieri motorcycle troops pauses for a drink. All the motorcycles are set to move off at a moment's notice with their carbines propped against them. The three Celere (Fast) divisions involved in the invasion of Yugoslavia included two battalions of motorcyclists with the *Eugenio De Savoia* Division. On the strength of the *Centauro* Armored Division there was also the 22nd Bersaglieri Motorcycle Battalion.

The Italian-Yugoslav border actually ran through the center of the city of Fiume-Sussak. Here Italian troops march into the Yugoslav town of Sussak where control had been disputed since the end of WWI. The Italian poet and patriot Garbiele d'Aunnuzio took over the town with 2000 armed followers in September 1919, hoping that Italy would annex it. When they refused to do so, he set up a short-lived independent republic that lasted until December 1920 in defiance of international law.

Soldiers of the *Messina* Infantry Division march into the center of the town of Cetinje in Montenegro during the April offensive. The men are wearing full kit with M1939 rucksacks instead of the standard infantry M1939 knapsack. Although generally used by the Alpini, the rucksack was also used in some cases by ordinary infantry. The *Messina* Division was to perform occupation duties in Montenegro until the Italian armistice in 1943.

An Alpini column of the 4th *Cuneense* Alpini Division advances through a Montenegrin village with their equipment and kit carried by mules. The *Cuneense* Division fought on the southern Albanian Front during the invasion as part of the 14th Army Corps and advanced northwest along the coast. Having fought in France in 1940 and then in Yugoslavia in 1941, the division was sent to Russia where it was destroyed in the 1943 Soviet Don offensive.

The band of a Bersaglieri cyclist unit plays in a newly occupied town in the Istrian region on the northern Dalmatian coast in April 1941. Bersaglieri regiments included three bicycle battalions, each of which had three bicycle companies and a motorcycle machinegun company. This region came under the control of Italy after Yugoslavia's defeat when the conquered country was divided up between Germany, Italy and Hungary, as well as the creation of the puppet state of Croatia.

An AB-41 armored car moves along a mountain road in Yugoslavia in 1942 while on anti-partisan duties. The AB-41 was a modern well-designed and relatively well-armed armored car with a 47mm main gun. It saw service on all fronts during the war. In the Balkans it was used for patrol and escort duties by the Bersaglieri and cavalry branches, a duty it did very effectively.

Infantry on an anti-partisan patrol fire across a fast-flowing river with their Breda-30 light machinegun on 25 May 1942. A large number of Italian troops were tied down in occupation duties in Yugoslavia, with most divisions not serving in Russia or North Africa in the fighting role.

These Montenegrin Chetnik volunteers of Captain Pavle Giuusic's commandos are pictured in a parade in September 1942 while serving under the loose control of the Italian MVAC organization. This unit was part of Colonel Bajo Stanisic's National Army of Montenegro and Herzegovina, which was made up of six nationalist battalions that included some Chetnik units. Their skull-and-crossbones flag was a typical Chetnik standard during WWII, whether fighting against the Italians or Germans, or as often was the case, cooperating with them against the partisans. In 1941-43, Italian occupation forces attempted to raise anti-communist volunteers from amongst the Slovenian, Montenegrin and Dalmatian populations of Yugoslavia. These anti-communist volunteers were recruited from every religious and ethnic group, and more often than not, their motives for fighting were nothing to do with being pro-Italian or German.

At the same parade an Italian officer inspects a Chetnik unit mainly dressed in ex-Royal Yugoslav Army uniforms and festooned with cartridge belts. MVAC troops were armed initially with ex-Yugoslav rifles and machineguns before being supplied with some Italian weaponry later on.

Slovenian MVAC White Guard troops on parade with a unit of Italian soldiers before going on anti-partisan duties in 1942. The White Guard and other Slovenian militias such as the Legion of Death were made up of anti-communists who volunteered to fight partisans. White Guards wore black berets with skull-and-crossbones badges and a mix of civilian, ex-Yugoslav and Italian tunics. In late 1942 some White Guards were issued with surplus ex-Italian Army tropical tunics worn with the usual black beret.

Truck-mounted mountain artillery of the Alpini set out on an anti-partisan operation in Yugoslavia in 1942. The 75mm 75/13 mountain gun was an outdated WWI design that served the Italian Army throughout the war. Three Alpini divisions - the *Pusteria*, *Taurinense* and *Alpi Graie* - served on occupation duties in Yugoslavia at various times during the war, and were always at the forefront of any anti-partisan operations.

Having unloaded their 75mm 75/13 mountain guns from their trucks, these Alpini are moving them into position. The men in shirt-sleeve order have added sprigs of foliage to their Alpini hats in an effort to camouflage them. (James Burd)

Outside a barracks in occupied Yugoslavia, an Alpini officer stands amidst a motorcycle bodyguard unit waiting to escort a high-ranking officer. The motorcyclists are wearing out-of-date M1916 steel helmets instead of the more usual leather crash helmet. These old-style steel helmets were still worn in 1940-43 by antiaircraft gun crews, and were brought out of storage to be worn by second-line coastal divisions up till 1943.

A mortar crew and infantry escort move out on patrol in an anti-partisan drive in Slovenia in the summer of 1942. This operation, which began in July, was to employ four Italian divisions as well as other attached units and Slovenian White Guard volunteers.

Soldiers with their Breda 30 light machinegun shelter behind a hastily erected protective stone wall while on an anti-partisan operation. Italian troops were heavily involved in most anti-partisan operations during the occupation and suffered heavy casualties. From 1941-43, they lost about 9000 killed and more than 15,000 wounded, with a further 6000 missing in action.

Soldiers troop through the thickly wooded terrain of Yugoslavia in the morning gloom while on anti-partisan operations. The Italians took part in several large-scale anti-partisan operations in 1941-43 alongside German allies and local volunteers. Resistance involving thousands of former Royal Yugoslav soldiers began in July 1941, and the cause was soon taken up by Tito and his communist partisans. Repressive measures taken by Germans made Italy's task of policing the region much more difficult.

A six-man infantry patrol in Yugoslavia moves cautiously across a frozen road leaving them exposed to attack. Apart from small-scale patrols like this, the Italians were involved in a series of large-scale anti-partisan operations from 1941-43. Operation Schwarz, for instance, included the *Ferrara*, *Venezia*, *Murge* and *Perugia* Infantry Divisions and the *Taurinense* Alpini Division. In total this operation involved 127,000 Germans, Italians and Bulgarians, as well as Croatian and Chetnik troops.

A machinegun section moves forward to operate their Breda M37 medium machinegun during training for anti-partisan operations in Yugoslavia. Two riflemen are preparing to give covering fire with their Carcano carbines, while the loader crawls forward with spare 20-round clips for the M37.

Russian Front, 1941-43

During the Russian summer of 1941, a happy column of Italian infantry marches to the front from their concentration areas in Rumania. If the Italians were lucky, they had a six-day train journey from Italy to Romanian disembarkation points, and then a 300km march to the concentration area. These men are wearing gray fatigue uniforms in an effort to preserve their gray-green uniforms for frontline service.

Two Bersaglieri radio operators wearing gray fatigue uniforms use a Model RF2 radio carried in the back of a Benelli motor-tricycle combination on the Ukrainian steppes. In the distance a long column of Italian infantry advances through cornfields as they make their way to the front.

Cavalry ride past the camera on their way to the front where they served with distinction in several engagements. Two cavalry regiments, the *Savoia* and the *Lancieri Di Novaro*, served on the Eastern Front as part of the *Principe Amadeo Duca d'Aosta* Celere (Fast) Division. An Italian cavalry regiment comprised 37 officers, 37 NCOs and 798 men with 818 horses, as well as six motorcycles, 16 trucks and 39 bicycles.

Two Bersaglieri motorcyclists armed with Carcano carbines with folding bayonets ride in tandem towards the frontline during the summer of 1941. This photograph shows to good effect the cockerel feathers adorning their helmets. With their proud tradition, the Bersaglieri have worn this headgear adornment in combat throughout their history.

During the Italian advance through southern Russia in the summer of 1941, this smartly dressed sapper company marches to the front. The gray-green uniform of the Italian soldier did not usually retain this well-kept appearance for long when marching through the dust of the hot Russian summer. Engineer insignia is shown by the red-edged, black flame superimposed over the divisional patch.

Infantry run at full speed across open ground as they advance through the outskirts of a Ukrainian town. The men have left most of their equipment in the rear and only have their cotton tactical bags to carry spare ammunition.

The crew of a 75mm 75/27 Model 11 field gun brings it into action on the Russian Front in August 1941. Although this French-designed gun was quite advanced when it first entered service in 1911, it was obsolete by 1940. Nevertheless, 1800 were still in use with the Italian Army at the outbreak of war, and it continued in service until 1943.

The crew of a 75/27 Model 1911 field gun digs a firing pit for their gun during fighting in the Ukraine in 1941. This artillery piece saw widespread service with the Italian Army in Russia, with 48 guns in the CSIR arsenal. With the expansion of the CSIR into the 8th Army in 1942, the number of 75/27 guns rose to 72.

On the edge of a Russian cornfield a 47/32 antitank gun crewed by Bersaglieri from one of the Celere (Fast) divisions of the CSIR is readied for action in August 1941. The 47/32 was a reasonably effective weapon with a high rate of fire, but it was not potent enough against new Soviet tanks appearing in Russia in 1941-42. Its lack of a shield made the gun's crew highly vulnerable to enemy small arms and shell fire.

Italian soldiers climb all over a disabled Soviet BT-7 medium tank destroyed in an earlier action. The BT-7 was the main medium tank of the Soviet Army before the introduction of the famous T-34/76. Any war-booty Soviet tanks taken by the Italians on the Eastern Front were usually used by the unit that had captured them. In total the Italians captured 14 armored vehicles on the Eastern Front, including several BT-7s, T-34/76s and a few light tanks, as well as a Katyusha multiple rocket launcher.

...oldiers curiously examine a Soviet Sukhoi Su-2 light bomber destroyed by Italian antiaircraft fire on the Don Front. This type of Russian bomber was replaced ...y the far more successful Ilyushin Il-2 Shturmovik dive-bomber from 1942 onwards. The Italians sent a small air contingent, the *Corpo Aereo Spedizione,* to ...e Russian Front. It was made up of the 22nd Fighter Group and 61st Reconnaissance Group.

An Italian supply convoy waits at a Don River crossing in Russia to bring up badly needed supplies for the CSIR. Italian trucks were not always robust enough for the terrible road conditions encountered on the Russian Front. Mechanical breakdowns accentuated a preexistent shortage of trucks, and this led to drastic measures being taken to try and solve the problem. Vehicles were taken from regimental depots and formed into centralized motor units that were then formed into ad hoc supply columns.

...his supply column on the River Don is ...ade up of camouflaged medium and ...eavy trucks towing trailers. In the ...reground is the escort for the column - a ...otorcyclist outrider and Fiat 108C field ...ar covered in camouflage netting. The ...08C was based on the Balilla car and was ...e of the more commonly used field cars ... the Italian Army. It was produced ...roughout the war.

A medal presentation ceremony held
Carlowska on the Don River
November 1941 features soldiers fro
several branches of the Italian Arm
who have just received awards. To th
left of the group are three Bersaglie
one a sergeant major the other tw
privates. Next in line is a corporal maj
of artillery, and then finally an office
and sergeant major of infantry from th
Pasubio Infantry Division. Th
Bersaglieri are easily identified by th
black cockerel feathers in the
helmets, while the artilleryman has th
brown leather bandolier used by h
branch of the army.

This Breda 30 light machinegun crew
prepares to fire their weapon from an
extremely exposed position on a frozen
Ukrainian river in December 1941. The
Breda was a poor design with the
innovative interchangeable barrel
needing to be replaced every 250
rounds when fired rapidly. Every round
from the Breda's 20-round clip was
lubricated with oil as it went into the
chamber, this leading to jams when the
mechanism was fouled with mud and
dirt. Its lack of a carrying handle,
combined with its sharp edges and hot
barrel, made it an uncomfortable
weapon to transport.

A Fiat 626N medium truck covered in camouflage netting moves into a
Ukrainian town alongside the main railway, while one of its crew runs
alongside. On the left-hand side at the front of the truck is the white-winged
wheel symbol of the motor transport corps in use since 1936.

Two infantrymen fire from behind a snowdrift during fighting on the Don Fro
in the winter of 1941. Both men wear the standard Model 1934 singl
breasted greatcoat, which was inadequate for use in most winters, nev
mind the extreme temperatures faced in Russia. Underneath their helme
they wear either regulation woolen caps or bustina side caps - or perha
both together to afford some warmth! One of the men has acquired
captured Soviet Mosin-Nagant M1891 rifle with its bayonet fixed, a weapo
of similar vintage to the standard Italian Carcano 1891.

The crew of a 47mm 47/32 antitank gun huddles in their inadequate clothing to wait for the next Soviet attack in 1942. Even though the 47mm gun was not potent enough against most Allied armor by this date, it was the best the Italians had available. Its crew is keeping warm as best they can in the extreme temperatures, though with only their poor-quality single-breasted greatcoats, balaclavas and gloves, they must be suffering.

An officer and NCO of a Bersaglieri regiment distribute mail and other packages using a traditional Russian sleigh pulled by two disheveled-looking *panje* horses. Like their German allies, the Italians had to adapt to the conditions they faced on the Russian Front using whatever forms of transport were available.

When the CSIR went to Russia in 1941, the 75/27 Model 1912 field gun being loaded here by its crew made up the strength of the horse-drawn artillery regiment. This regiment had been formed from artillery groups of the 1st and 2nd Celere Divisions. The artillery group of the 3rd Division *Principo Amede Duca d'Aosta* was also attached to the latter. When the 8th Army (or ARMIR) was formed in 1942, the 75/27 Model 12 was replaced with two groups of 75/27 Model 11 guns and one group of 100/17 howitzers.

An infantry captain hands mail to one of his men in a posed photograph intended to keep up the spirits of families of Italians serving on the Eastern Front. Longsuffering Italian soldiers were fortunate if they received much in the way of home comforts. This man is fortunate to at least be issued with a Romanian-type *ciacula* fur hat that was not standard issue.

Alpini of the *Monte Cervino* Ski Battalion in training with their 47mm antitank guns before being issued with white snowsuits. In the meantime, they have been issued with white covers for their steel helmets, and white canvas cartridge belts worn with the standard gray-green uniform. The gun has its carriage wheels removed for firing and its crew is going about its assigned duties. In the foreground is a corporal major aimer and crew commander.

Alpini of the *Monte Cervino* Ski Battalion camouflaged in white take a break as they warm themselves around a hastily built fire. Their skis are close at hand and their Carcano M1891 carbines are slung over their shoulders in readiness. *Monte Cervino* arrived in Russia in February 1942 as reinforcements for the CSIR. They soon gained a good reputation as a well-trained and well-equipped unit, even gaining the grudging respect of their German allies.

A soldier of the *Monte Cervino* Alpini Ski Battalion pulls on thick winter gloves as he prepares for sentry duty. He is well equipped for the cold with a white camouflage suit worn over the gray-green uniform, and a cloth cover for his helmet. The large canvas over-boots are well insulated and would be essential to stop him suffering frostbite. Unfortunately for the average Italian soldier in Russia, special winter clothing was largely restricted to special units like *Monte Cervino*, who were also lucky to be issued with boots with insulated vibram soles.

Alpini drivers maneuver around a marsh in Autocaretta OM Model 32 vehicles on the Russian Front. Italian supply lines were as vulnerable to partisan attack as their German allies, and the whole of the *Vicenza* Infantry Division was used in rear areas on lines-of-communication duties.

The crew of a Breda 20/65 20mm antiaircraft gun brings their weapon into action in a town on the Don Front in February 1942. Although the Breda was a very useful weapon, by 1942 its effectiveness in the antiaircraft role was lessening as most combat aircraft were better armored. In the antitank role, however, the Breda was still a useful weapon and could penetrate most armored cars at 600m.

This photograph shows what is probably a staged reenactment of a heroic engagement on 15 February 1942, where troopers of the *Savoia* Cavalry Regiment charged across the Isbuschenski steppes. In this famous action, 600 unsupported men of the *Savoia* charged a Soviet unit of 2000 infantry with artillery support. The *Savoia* caught the enemy completely by surprise and swept the three Soviet battalions off the battlefield, taking 500 prisoners, four field guns, 50 machineguns and ten mortars. As well as being one of the last ever cavalry charges in history, the victory was one of the few occasions in modern warfare when cavalry alone defeated an infantry force supported by machineguns and artillery.

A Lancia 3RO heavy truck of 34d Autoreparto Pesante (34th Heavy Truck Company) transporting five mules to the front is dug out of a rut in a muddy road. This truck type first used in Ethiopia in 1935-36 could carry a substantial load of 32 men or seven horses or mules. They could also carry light tanks. As one of the main workhorses of the Italian Army supply system, a total of 8656 3RO trucks were built in 1940-43. The 34th Heavy Truck Company, along with the 33rd, 96th and 97th Companies, made up the 29th Heavy Truck Battalion of the CSIR.

The two-man crew of a Lanciafiamme Model 40 portable flamethrower fires their weapon against a Russian position. The Model 40 weighed 27kg and could only be carried short distances. It was capable of shooting an 18m-long flame for up to a maximum of 12 seconds. The operator wore a protective suit and gasmask while his assistant, whose job it was to protect him, wore a standard uniform.

The flag party of the Italian Croatian Legion parade their unit's flag en-route to the Italian Army on the Russian Front in April 1942. Croatians recruited from the coastal regions of their newly independent nation formed a two-battalion MVSN legion with an artillery battalion to serve with the Italian 8th Army. With a strength of 1215 men, the legion known as the Legione Croata Autotransportabile served with the Italian 3rd Mobile Division, but was destroyed during the retreat from the Don Front in December 1942.

Cossack volunteers of the *Savoia Gruppo* attached to the Italian Army on the Eastern Front celebrate in their usual exuberant manner. Italy recruited a small 360-strong unit of these Russian volunteers to act as scouts for their army. They were of course following the example of Germany, who employed thousands of Russian nationals in auxiliary roles on the Eastern Front. The only insignia worn by the Cossacks of the *Savoia Gruppo* was a tricolor chevron worn on the left sleeve of the traditional *Tcherkesska* tunic.

General Giovanni Messe, commander of the Italian CSIR in 1941-42, inspects soldiers who have been in action on the Don Front. General Messe was commander until replaced by General Italo Garibaldi in the summer of 1942. Garibaldi took over command as the CSIR was expanded by the addition of seven new divisions into the renamed 8th Army.

General Messe inspects a trench with his entourage. Before taking over leadership of the CSIR, Messe had commanded an army corps during the invasion of Greece and had proved an able commander, though his background in armored and motorized warfare might have made him more useful to the Italian war effort in North Africa. In January 1943 he took over command of Axis forces in Tunisia where he again proved to be one of Italy's best generals.

Engineers work on the construction of a camouflaged bunker in a newly captured position in the Don Basin in September 1942. The improvised roof of the shelter appears to be reinforced with metal from sections of a pontoon bridge. Rubble was then piled on top of the roof and covered with the camouflage netting in the background.

Soldiers dragging a 47mm Cannone da 47/32 M35 antitank gun and its ammunition move at the double along a railway line on the Don Front in the lat summer of 1942. The men have Carcano carbines slung over their backs, and carry the barest of equipment with Type 35 gasmask bags. In many cases th gasmask would have been discarded and the bag then used as an improvised hold-all by soldiers.

A sapper armed with a Carcano TS carbine attempts to remove a Sovie mine during a mine-clearing operation. The Italian Army ordered 20,000 T carbines in 8mm caliber instead of the standard 6.5mm for service on th Russian Front. However, the vicious recoil produced by the larger round le to them being withdrawn from service.

War booty taken by Italians in Russia included a Soviet 122mm field gun, and rather surprisingly, a pair of Siberian camels captured by the *Val Chiese* Alpini Battalion. Mules and horses were more common draught animals but these exotic creatures were obviously used by the Russians as well. All Axis armies on the Russian Front relied heavily on horse-drawn transport, so Italians would no doubt have utilized these camels as did their Romanian allies.

A German general presents the Iron Cross to a colonel of the *Torino* Division in Russia, while brother officers look on. The relationship between Italian and German officers was often strained. German arrogance towards Italians at all levels caused great resentment, and the latter constantly complained their ally did not take them seriously. Conversely, Germans were frustrated by such things as Italy's insistence on promoting the status of what were basically infantry divisions (like *Torino* and *Pasubio*) by calling them motorized when they were clearly nothing of the sort.

In a useful propaganda photo opportunity for the Italian press, soldiers of the *Torino* Infantry Division feed Russian children. The Italians, with a more tolerant racial attitude to the Russians, were more likely to treat ordinary peasants with greater humanity than the Germans.

Umberto, Prince of Piedmont and heir to the Italian throne, inspects a unit of Alpini artillery about to leave for the Russian Front. Although Umberto held military command during the war and was officially commanding officer during the campaign against the French in June 1940, he was never a supporter of the Mussolini regime. The prince's rank of General of the Army is shown by the insignia on his greatcoat sleeve. All artillerymen have bayonets fixed to their artillery-pattern TS Carcano carbines.

Italian infantry throw gifts to crews of passing German Pz.Kpfw. III tanks on their way to the frontline, while others shake hands with them in a show of solidarity for the propaganda camera. The relationship between Italians and Germans was often not so friendly with a lot of distrust on both sides. This mutual dislike stemmed mainly from the lack of respect shown to Italian soldiers by German officers and men.

A platoon advances past a forlorn-looking *panje* horse towards a railway junction on the outskirts of a Ukrainian town. As the Italian advance continued through the Ukraine in 1941-42, temperatures dropped to -20°C and the badly clothed soldiers suffered terribly. Italians and their Hungarian and Romanian counterparts were often blamed unfairly by Hitler for failures on the Russian Front. Unlike the Romanians and Hungarians, who attempted to resist Hitler's demand for more troops, Mussolini had no problem with sending additional forces to Russia when Hitler asked him to do so in 1942.

This soldier armed with a Carcano M91 rifle with fixed bayonet has wrapped himself up as well as he can to try and stave off the bone-chilling cold. As with all combatants fighting in Russia, woolen items knitted by Italian womenfolk at home supplemented inadequate issue winter clothing. The Fascist PNF imitated German winter relief campaigns and organized collection points at local party offices for people to donate woolen and other winter clothing.

A platoon of infantry halts and takes cover during an advance into the industrial suburb of a Russian town. Although the CSIR, and its successor the 8th Army, took a number of towns in house-to-house fighting during their advance into Russia, they were saved the horror of fighting for Stalingrad alongside the German 6th Army. However, when the Soviets launched their offensive to cut off the 6th Army in late 1942, the Italians, Hungarians and Romanians holding the flanks for the Germans were to suffer terribly.

An 81mm Model 35 mortar crew prepares their weapon as one man adjusts the sights. The Model 35 was based on the French Brandt design. Two weights of bomb were fired by the Model 35 - the 7.2lb type had a range of 4052m, while the 15.1lb round had a range of 1500m. This compared favorably with the Soviet 82mm equivalent, which only had a range of 3100m.

Having used stones to build a bunker for protection, this team from a Bersaglieri regiment fires their Breda Model 37 medium machinegun. In the bitter cold of a Russian winter, the firer wears woolen gloves to stop his hands freezing to the trigger. The Model 37 was a good weapon with few of the faults associated with other Italian machineguns in service.

Alpini ski troops on patrol in a snowy wood are well camouflaged in their white snowsuits. They are dragging supplies behind them on an improvised sledge. The Alpini were highly trained mountain troops and were really wasted in the infantry role they had as part of the CSIR/8th Army on the frozen steppes.

Struggling through the winter is a column of improvised wooden supply carts resting on sledges from a traditional sleigh and pulled by *panje* ponies. The soldier helping to move the sleigh with the slung carbine is wrapped up in whatever items of uniform and civilian gear he could find.

With their drivers wrapped up against the biting cold, a motorized column slowly moves towards the front. At the front and rear of the column are two Pavesi Model 1930 artillery tractors with their drivers exposed to the freezing conditions. In between the tractors is a Lancia 3Ro heavy truck with a soldier hitching an uncomfortable ride on a running board. Italy's lack of motor transport was not helped by the fact that the war ministry did not supply low-temperature lubricants for vehicles!

50

The rider of a Benelli cargo motor-tricycle examines the contents of a care package from home as he sits on his vehicle in 1942. These useful light vehicles were manufactured during the 1930s by Benelli and Moto Guzzi, and were also sometimes fitted with machineguns. This soldier has been issued with the Romanian-style *ciacula* fur hat, which was often bought by the Italian commissariat because of shortages of official winter headgear.

brigadier general, colonel and other officers gather around captured Soviet 45mm antitank gun and limber to discuss merits. Italians would have been grateful for any captured oviet weaponry but there is not much evidence of their using tillery and tanks to the same extent as Germany.

talian soldiers prepare to tow a captured Soviet 45mm antitank gun using a native Russian *panje* sledge. Axis armies in Russia employed these sledges in he winter when they found their trucks could not move on impassable Russian roads.

Italians fortified captured Russian villages in an effort to counter the Soviet Army's superiority in armor and artillery. Individual houses were turned int improvised fortresses and this Bersaglieri machine gunner is firing his Breda 30 light machinegun from behind the wall of one such position. He is at leas well dressed for the conditions as he waits alone for the next Soviet attack. Spare clips for his weapon are on the wall.

Two Italian 149mm Canone de 149/40 Model 35 field guns ready to fire fror their dug-in positions in 1941-42. This field gun first produced in 1934 wa one of the few modern artillery pieces in service with the Italian Army WWII. The priority given to the Russian Front by Mussolini is shown by th fact that there were 36 of these guns in Russia and only 12 in service North Africa.

On 26 January 1943, the Italian Army fought a desperate battle at Nikolajewka, led mainly by the *Tridentina* Alpini Division, where it managed to break through the encircling Soviet Army. This long column of survivors from the battle is withdrawing towards a new defensive line established by the Germans. After this engagement the Italian Army on the Eastern Front was virtually destroyed as a fighting force and so was evacuated back to Italy. This left only a token Italian military presence in Russia that fought on until the armistice in September.

CONCORD
PUBLICATIONS COMPANY

ISBN 962-361-150-1

0 89195 26520 3

T3-BJJ-106

Waffen-SS

(2) From Glory to Defeat 1943-1945

Robert Michulec & Ronald Volstad

CONCORD

PUBLICATIONS COMPANY